Counting the Waves

Counting the Waves

Poems by Deborah Cummins

Word Press

Published by Word Press
P.O. Box 541106
Cincinnati, OH 45254-1106

Typeset in Aldine by WordTech Communications LLC,
Cincinnati, OH

ISBN: 1933456302
LCCN: 2006927689

Poetry Editor: Kevin Walzer
Business Editor: Lori Jareo

Visit us on the web at www.word-press.com

Acknowledgments

Grateful acknowledgment is made to the editors of the following publications where some of these poems previously appeared, a few in somewhat different versions:

Ascent: "Just One God"
Crab Orchard Review: "The Season's First Apples," "Dawn"
Connecticut Review: "Take It or Leave It"
Louisiana Literature: "Before It's Too Late"
Michigan Quarterly Review: "So Many Depictions"
New England Review: "If Not Moonless," "Trompe L'Oeil"
Ninth Letter: "Apple Tree," "Winter Kill"
Orion: "Encounter"
Rhino: "Another Life"
Runes: "When Spring Is Late to the Garden"
Shenandoah: "The Body's Betrayals"
Sou'Wester: "Leaving the Grocery Store at Sunset," "Keys"
The Spoon River Poetry Review: "In the Neighborhood"
Tar River Poetry: "Island Wave," "Slow Children," "The Question"
TriQuarterly: "Tidy," "Why Insist"
The Yale Review: "From a Third Floor Window in Bogliasco"

"Tidy" also appeared in *Poetry Calendar 2006* (Alhambra Publishing, Brussels)

I am deeply grateful to Andrea Hollander Budy, Susan Hahn, and Kathleen Lynch for their valuable insights, generosity and rigor in helping to shape many of these poems.

I owe much appreciation to the Virginia Center for the Creative Arts and the Bogliasco Foundation for their periods of residence during which a number of these poems were written. Many thanks, also, to the Illinois Arts Council for their continuing recognition and support.

For their gifts of joy and wonder, I owe many thanks to my grandchildren and Michael. A special thanks is also owed my parents, for the safe haven where books were always welcome.

Finally, my deepest gratitude goes to Bob for his wisdom, humor and unwavering encouragement, and for sharing the journey.

For Christina

sister, friend —

Contents

Inheritance

A morning of dew and sky and incoming tide,
of a broad-armed maple holding forth
on its palm the first orange leaf.
Geese unzip the horizon.
Rafts of migrant seabirds gorge.

Tranquil glories. So simple
and complex, my not desiring
a single other thing, not wanting
to be anywhere else. Once
lots must've been drawn,

and by chance, I drew well.
The others? The throw-away boys,
broken girls, the old alone men
and bent, bitter women?
This isn't about them.

This isn't about absence or lost promise,
about wars or multitudes, droughts or floods.
Nor the mistaken notion
that the rich—however measured—
have an obligation to be happy.

On this about-to-be-golden morning,
there's no other civilization but this one.
I lament nothing.
Later perhaps, for some foolishness
or silence or intentional cruelty,

I may ask to be forgiven.

For now, I embark into the day,
my luggage light—some nouns,
a peppering of verbs—all I need.
And the landscape, too, lacks nothing.

Except for, with me in it, my responsibility—
ah, here's the obligation—
to look and look.

I.

Encounter

So you think yourself powerful
when you walk to pier's end
and your mere shadow drives minnows
by the hundreds out of the shallows.
On the deck, you turn a page of your book,
and the hummingbird deep in the fuchsia's neck
blurs, whirring off.
At dawn, your strolling the same lane
as the doe is enough
to startle her retreat into the thick, dark spruce.
These could have been my thoughts
but were not, as I swung in the hammock,
tired or lazy on an August afternoon.
Perhaps I resembled a slumbering beast
to the swallowtail who flitted above
and alighted, to my astonishment,
on my bare forearm, rested there
in her wild unremembering.
With one swack, I could've ended her
or sent her away. Just lifting my head
would've done the trick.
But I didn't blink, draw a deep breath
as she fanned her wings, probed
my skin as delicately as an eyelash
brushes a cheek. Again,
the surprise was mine
when—nothing more—she rose, disappeared
into the trees, and stirred in me a yearning
against which I was powerless.

Apple Tree

"And what times are these, when
To speak of trees is almost a crime
Because it implies silence about so many
injustices?"

                                        Bertolt Brecht

Forgive us our pre-occupation
with a fifty-year-old apple tree, its uprooted
thirty-five-foot spread transported by flatbed
along Route 3, the entire length of the peninsula.

Forgive us our outrage
at the state trooper's escort, the flanking
utility trucks raising power lines, a 3 m.p.h. entourage
halting traffic for hours, no detours permitted.

Allow us our week's worth of front page coverage,
of who in what office is to blame,
and who among the taxpayers
missed work or school, a doctor's appointment

or the ferry to Swan's Island for a funeral.
Look kindly on the op-eds
redefining conspicuous consumption
as a man with a new garden and will and money

to plant anything he can, although why then
for such a transplant didn't he enlist
helicopter or barge. And forgive me
who's merely enchanted now

by the fuss, by the improbable journey
of one innocent apple tree,
its broad limbs and nodding branches
riding that flatbed like a queen

waving from a homecoming float—
just as I forgive a God
who most days only checks in, listens
to how things are getting on,

doesn't intervene, doesn't offer
a cure, miracle or banishment,
which, actually, sometimes at least,
seems exactly appropriate.

When Spring is Late to the Garden

Already I want midsummer, that old intoxicant
frothing with pith and sap,
when everything seems possible,
even life without end.

I've watched you thinking it, too, leaning,
dreamy, into your rake.
Sweet accomplice, how gently you brush away
the flowerbed's detritus, capitulations to winter,

the season it's easy to know despair.
But the wind's sudden rise reminds me
of the beauty in bare trees,
their dip and sway. And the light

no longer so indifferent, finds your sleeve,
claims your bent back, as furtive
then certain as Eve's reach must've been,
the whole limb snapping down.

More slowly, after, it must have come to them—
the consequence that something had changed
or was about to, their wondering
Why? and *When?* the very questions

that, as you straighten, turn in my direction,
seem poised on your lips. As if,
through improbable linkage, I were responsible
for this cold, these small green unravelings.

If a Single Word

I once thought that a single word
had the power to change.
To transform.

Eavan Boland

If a single word has the power to transform,
I'd have to propose *choice*.
I'd have to consider how Lot's wife turned back,
her small glance all she needed,
knowing where to look among the towers for her house
where once she sang, spun cloth.
Tonight, walking the streets of my neighborhood,
I must consider as well my ancestral mothers
who delivered me here, who, after
their trunks were stowed, all children
accounted for, stood at the railing and watched
the shores of their homeland recede.
Here, where I live, no street name or sign or yard
is unfamiliar. I'm free
to contemplate every aspect of shadow
as darkness descends early in late autumn,
free to stand here on my small piece of ground,
considering my house's open door, its windows
lit against the night, and, if not transformed,
know gratitude, adding *mine*.

Trompe L'Oeil

A house's painted window
with shutters and latch, white curtains,
a potted geranium on the sill,
shadows that never lengthen,
never, beneath clouds, disappear.

The eye knows a lie, or maybe it doesn't.
These rendered blooms
don't need water, never wilt.
And what of the stone sill itself?
Imagine a cat sunning there,

batting dead flies, lapping a saucer of milk.
Consider how furtively
a woman might peek from those parted curtains
in a window that needs no key for its latch,
no oil to quiet its hinge.

The eye is a willing accomplice,
embraces artifice when it serves
symmetrical balance,
appreciates the way windows line up
with such a painted addition, an equal number

on either side of the door.
Or, with the dumb trust of a slobbering retriever
willing to chase the same stick
over and over, the eye sees
what it needs to believe,

maintains a willed innocence,

even when evidence proves contrary—
as when the doctor points to a dark
unremarkable shadow on your X-ray
and the eye takes it in

as a monochrome, some abstracted study
of snow in a blizzard or the sea in fog,
everything obscured.
This time, the trick of the eye required:
what isn't there.

Counting the Waves

Overheard at the island's market:
Child: "I'm bored."
Mother: "Go count the waves."

Better than watching paint dry.
Or grass grow. Although if it sprouted
in a meadow with a broad-armed maple,
some drowsy bees, swaying rue....
There are worse ways to occupy time.
Consider Sisyphus.
Or imagine a mother with higher aspirations
who directs: "Roll back the waves.
Eradicate the tides."

Maybe impossible challenges are desired,
unreasonable expectations.
Not the sheep we count to slumber
but that needle in the salt hay.
Or the attempt to glue back on trees
a tumult of fallen October leaves.

"Go count the waves,"
a mother solemnly intones, and somewhere
beneath a high, hot sun, a child might obey,
discovering, as he loses count, the waves'
myriad glittery eyes.
Or he attends then to the beach's sand, each grain
more minute than the head of a pin, upon which—
remind me—how many angels dance?

If Not Moonless

after Margaret Gibson

Hours ago, the day bid its final goodnight—
pale strip on the horizon, small
hankie fluttered from a receding ship.
Lines blurred, the firred woods a smudge,
the pond a smear. Now, dark,
slurried with clouds but not really moonless,
night attempts erasure, and sounds awaken,
as though to a trumpet call, shrill, clarion.

Aloft, an owl announces itself.
Long past vespers, frogs in the creekbed's clay
raise their mortal chorus.
And just as a pool's current to be seen
requires branch or rock to eddy around,
last season's lingering beech leaves, their restless quake,
give shape to wind, make of it
something tangible, solid.
Obedient, rapt, I listen.

But tonight, if not *moonless,*
occluded? Or is *obliterated* more accurate?
Why need words at all? Among these gifts
dished up every night, why require
the clatter of syllables or some equivalent cry
in a language I can understand?

On this lane to the pond, small rise over the field,
a mere month after his death, so sudden and violent,
I still, in silence or inarticulate racket,

yearn for words with their power to tell me
if this wind touching my face, my throat's hollow
is one part of a singular wind
that, long and unbroken, travels the earth
with no beginning or end.
Tonight's wind, I must believe,
has not been effaced,
has not been removed or destroyed or shut off.
Obfuscated, I have faith, is more apt.

Above Sant' Ilario

April 2004

Up this high, the ground is dry,
rock-strewn, the soil all lime.
Wind has stooped a few cypress, pine,
a small grove of olive.

Wildflowers stipple a field,
rosemary perfumes the smell of hard labor.
Somewhere below, a goat bleats, a dog unsettles
the afternoon's repose.

Soon, behind the stone walls
and pulled shutters I passed climbing,
there'll be trowels clinking in gardens,
a rattle of dishes being cleared.

Up here, the mossy steps and narrow *caruggi* end.
Ancient paths twist toward the ridge's bouldered spine.
I'm centuries removed
from these high-altitude defenses

against marauding Saracens, though the view
of the sea, save for a few white sails,
a freighter putting out from Genoa harbor,
may be little changed. The invasion

I'm evading, an intentional detachment,
is from the world a world away from this one,
but to which, as the *chiesa's* tolling
ratchets down the day,

I'll have to return, assaulted
by more news of myriad, senseless acts.
May it be gradual, come as slowly
as the snake I saw on yesterday's hike

which might be the type to slowly
devour a vole, the unhinged jaw
taking it whole, the vole
kicking, jerking,

then with a spasm, going limp,
a lump inch by inch
engorging the snake's full length.
Horrible, and necessary.

Near-Misses

*A terracotta impediment from a Chicago
high-rise plummeted 30 stories, slamming
through the roof of a car stopped in an
intersection. It sheered off the car's rear half,
missing the driver by inches.*

One more screw-up, another
in a string of near-misses, countless mistakes,
in spite of death's long experience,
its many allies equipped
with claw, talon, fang and web,
not to mention humankind's helpful assists,
how, like clockwork, we deliver
border skirmishes, territorial claims,
wars in the name of someone holy.
For every vaccine and cure, we offer
another nuclear warhead or toxic spill
or one more psychopathic misfit.
For every bullet that grazes a cheek,
there's umpteen times as much *collateral damage*.
In fact, if you think about it, death
has friends in every corner—
drought, disease, any number of malignancies.

Still, there's so much about death that isn't deadly.
It bungles, leaves behind in its sorry wake
the crippled, the confused and lost,
the tortured body as vessel of pain.
How much practice does it take to get it right?
Don't ask the car's driver or the woman
who escaped a Beretta held to her head.

Don't inquire of the passengers
who, after the emergency landing,
stumble, dazed, into the light.
Let's let them celebrate
death's mistake, think their immortal thoughts,
forgetting, if only for a moment,
that no matter the number of errors,
death, always the last to bat,
winds up winning.

Just One God

after Wesley McNair

And so many of us.
How can we expect Him
to keep track of which voice
goes with what request.
Words work their way skyward.
Oh Lord, followed by petition—
for a cure, the safe landing.
For what is lost, missing –
a spouse, a job, the final game.
Complaint cloaked as need –
the faster car, porcelain teeth.
That so many entreaties
go unanswered
may say less about our lamentable
inability to be heard
than our inherent flawed condition.

Why else, at birth, the first sound
we make, that full-throttled cry?
Of want, want, want.
Of never enough. Desire
as embedded in us as the ancestral tug
in my unconscienced dog who takes
to the woods, nose to the ground, pulled far
from domesticated hearth, bowl of kibble.
Left behind, I go about my superior business,
my daily ritual I could call prayer.

But look, this morning, in my kitchen,
I'm not asking for more of anything.

My husband slices bread,
hums a tune from our past.
Eggs spatter in a skillet.
Wands of lilac I stuck in a glass
by the open window wobble
in a radiant and—dare I say it? –
merciful light.

Leaving the Grocery Store at Sunset

So here's the sky once again showing off,
candling all that it touches
with a luminous glow: the interrupting
roofs and branches, poles and cables,
the 131 Express spewing its sooty fumes
and in this puddle-strewn parking lot,
my cart, tarnished chrome, iridesced.

How convincing the argument:
that our longing is to rise into such unearthly light.
But it's the sky, I maintain, that presses down,
needs our weighty abundance—
the cashier with her hair's glistening weave,
the stock boy uncrating bruised nectarines,
iced mackerel still able to gleam.

If the check-out lanes' headlines can be believed—
Dead Woman Awakes with Bracelet from Heaven—
then someone might have an answer.
Returned to this world's frictions and mess,
she might attest to the other's emptiness,
to the absence of all that *lush* or *pearly*
with which we seem enamored.

This woman who may have been there
and who's come back, if not with scientific proof
then data hard enough for the *National Enquirer*,
may see sunsets for what they are:
not potentially transforming events
but more attempts to pry loose our grips,
our hungry attachments that fill our baskets.

Oh sure, I see the sky's persuasive hues,
its sumptuous pink-bellied nimbus.
But I know how soon
they'll drag away the light, and leave it
to the stars with their connect-the-dot logic,
constellated efforts to limn the invisible
like so many jewels studding a bracelet.

From a Third Floor Window in Bogliasco

Nothing, today, is still.
Not the sea in its churning froth,
not the pine limbs or the rustling
potted hydrangeas on the sill.

The wind persists, the clouds
tack fast, like unfurled sails,
to the east. Gulls, with clamorous ease,
spread their wings and lift.

Another Sunday afternoon,
and nothing, it seems,
is without sound. Still
I know in any season

there is a silence,
the noiseless din
of what is lost or taken.
Another Sunday afternoon

and how gorgeous the world is,
the swallows' scattered flight,
wave cresting wave, the bells
striking the hours at Santa Maria.

There, the believers
in lace shawls and starched collars,
in spite of the air's agitation, spill
into the piazza, and brave

the *passeggiata a mare*,

the sea's indifferent spray.
Somewhere in this house, a shutter
has come undone.

It bangs and bangs, as though
it will never stop.
A door, unhinged,
swings wide open.

II.

Another Life

My mother, 18, the summer before she married,
lounges belly-down in the sun,
books and grass all around, her head on her hands
propped at a jaunty angle.
She smiles in a way I've never seen
at something beyond the camera.
This photograph I come back to again and again
invites me to re-write her life.
I keep resisting, certain
I'd have no part in it, her first born
though not exactly. A boy first,
two months premature, my brother
who lived three days, was buried in a coffin
my father carried. "The size of a shoe box,"
he said, the one time he spoke of it.
And my mother, too, offered only once
that she was pregnant and so they married.

Drawn to this saw-edged snapshot,
I'm almost convinced to put her in art school.
Single, she'd have a job in the city,
wouldn't marry. There'd be no children
if that would make her this happy.
But I'm not that unselfish, or stupid.
And what then, too, of my beloved sister,
her son I adore?

So let me just move her honeymoon
from the Wisconsin Dells to the Caribbean.
Let the occasional vacation in a Saugatuck cabin
be exactly what she wanted. The house

she so loved she won't have to sell.
Winters, there's enough money to pay the bills.
There are no cigarettes, no stroke, no paralysis.
Her right hand lifts a spoon from a bowl
as easily as if it were a sable-hair brush
to an empty canvas.
And the grass that summer day
on the cusp of another life
is thick, newly mown, fragrant.

Before It's Too Late

So at last I tell her to come out of the trees,
that I can't believe she's followed me
this time to central Virginia, to these hardwoods
at the edge of a hayfield overlooking a valley,
the Blue Ridge hunkered against the horizon.
Her voice of bitter complaint weaves in and out
of the leaves.
                    Before she gets to what-might've-been
had she married a smarter man,
and how of course I'd never understand
with my fatter wallet, my bigger house, I call
Come on, it isn't, as you always insist, too cold.
If the wind musses your hair, that, at least,
is easily fixed.
                    And though I never get back
whatever she must've said—or sung perhaps?—
withdrawing from my room, sleep hovering near,
the door ajar, a light in the hall reassuring,
I promise not to invent, again, another mother
who reads the classics or is happy
to walk the beach alone, stay up late with Mozart.
Before it's too late, I tell her
                              Come feel
the sun on your face. Watch how wind,
climbing this slope of unmown hay, carves absence.
Let's agree that hawk, looping the thermals,
fools no one it's just on a joy-ride.
Here's a log mapped with lichen
light hasn't touched yet. We can sit
at an easy distance, nothing between us.

In the Neighborhood

It was common knowledge—
Violet's father, a switchman at the yards,
lost his leg to a freight because he'd been tipping
the bottle, and old man DeGroot,
devoted churchman, beat his wife.

But I didn't know that Dick Delaney,
father of twins, excused himself
from supper, went out to the garage,
hung himself from the rafters,
that it wasn't his heart that gave out.

No one told me how
Suzy Rushton abused her adopted daughter
or what Clifford Sutton worked to perfect
with his bus driver's belt
behind his arbor vitae, his heavy drapes.

I could've used the truth
about our neighbors—when my family dropped
its public face of respect and good manners,
and behind closed doors, retreated
into insults, accusations,

each doused with expletives and broken dishes,
as if we hated each other, hated ourselves
in a bitter stretch of years
when our family enterprise, it seemed, propelled us,
yoked, toward some precipitous edge.

I needed Delaney, Rushton and Sutton then,

and later, the oldest Terwilliger sentenced to prison,
to help me understand my family,
how, in our loneliness and rage,
we were, relatively speaking, normal.

Take It or Leave It

at the dump's swap shed

Mary left a cabinet, took a chair.
Mike took the chair, left an iron skillet.
Robert hauled in a mattress, heaved the guts
of a washing machine onto his pick-up.
Now, a woman too young to look so old,
bends over a table heaped with cast-off,
Take-It clothes. Slowly she steps out
of her shoes, removes her purple blouse,
her blue pants. In her underwear,
she could be anyone.

But she's Marguerite whose daughter last month
drove off the bridge, who depends
on sleeping pills and gin, her reputation
for being *a little off*, a police record
of petty offense. I feign interest
in the paperbacks, a ragged copy
of, of all things, *Crime and Punishment*.
We endure a polite silence,
as though sitting in a library reading room.

Finally, empty-handed, the woman turns
from the table. She's so pale, she looks bled.
A safety pin holds up one strap of her bra.
Here, her lined face and flat eyes say,
is what I want to take: bad news
happening in some distant place.
Let me leave sleepless nights,
take finding my way in the dark,

leave suicidal water, take control at the wheel.
A change in name, a different
shake of the dice, and what is mine, her eyes say,
could've been hers.

She doesn't care that she violates
the swap shed's rituals of voluntary exchange,
how I don't want to claim
this burdensome unease her naked slouch
and sagging breasts demand.
Nor can I offer the right words to explain
I'm not blind to her longing
to disown, to dump heartache and cruel chance,
hoping that in the morning,
they'll be hauled away like trash.

Failing

Drawn to the margins between ebb and flood,
the woman wanders the shore below our bluff,
as I often do. She searches
low tide scatterings, bends and rises,
again and again, as though genuflecting at an altar
of driftwood and wrack, emptied
whelks and bivalves, things beautiful and dead.
I heard at the post office she lost her husband
in the twin towers, and after, failed
to succeed in killing herself.
They say "vaporized"
propelled her over the edge, not having,
at the end of the digging, one strand or chip,
the merest fragment. Hard to imagine
what gets prompted in her mind
by this September morning as blue
and gold as that one, by this shore's
detritus unable to minimize
the vast Atlantic, and our cobbled beach
with stones enough
to weight down anyone's pocket.

So Now I Have

after Linda Pastan

So now I have a Fire Road number,
a tin mailbox, a well and septic,

some winter blow-downs. I have
gulls and eiders, a cobbled beach.

My view, at ebb or flood, extends to Camden,
though in this morning's fog, no further

than the shoreline—who says
a paradise has to be perfect?

In this rite of opening the cottage,
of claiming another season, I feel

no obligation or expectation to be happy.
It's easy to speak of it casually.

I can almost trust the future,
shuck my fidelity to loss and grief.

I can almost forget
that every bright object throws a shadow,

that my having at last a house on the sea
is not some brief irrelevancy.

Still, how onerous this joy
a hand can bat away.

How you have and then you do not.

Meeting the Family

after Jan Bailey

Their Yankee faces beam.
They like to use *betrothed*.
Over stirred cocktails, Maine shrimp on toast,
they don't inquire so much as inform.
About seals and shags, the derivation of Down East.

Some one fetches a chart of the bay
studded with islands—Sprucehead, Eagle, Brimstone—
names the father claims she'll have to learn.
Pointing, her intended shows off
unmarked channels where, as a boy, he had to prove
his under-canvas mettle.
It's so much to fathom, she remarks,
and an aunt claps at the clever pun, proclaims
it's clear she'll soon be one of them.

At the table, bowls of shocked-open bivalves
relinquish their soft bodies.
In spite of the mother's numerous demonstrations—
the proper way, my dear, to dip—
there is, still, with each briny mouthful, grit
and after it, the indelicate business
of eating lobster. She fumbles to their amusement
with claw, tail, green tomali—the best part!—
all the while swimming against an impossible current
of discourse: hard-shells and shedders, ebb and flood,
knots and swells, the quaint and unendearing
customs of the natives.

Suddenly she yearns
for her land-locked Midwest, its flat prairies
and deciduous trees, common squirrels,
identifiable song birds, and, of all things, cows
with their limpid eyes, heads lowered
to fenced, cropped meadows.
With each swallow, her new life enters her
as if it were ballast. How lucky she is,
the brother exclaims, tomorrow's marine forecast:
unlimited visibility.
As if there were such a thing.
As if she hasn't, already,
seen so much, so soon.

"Divorce Yard Sale—Two Blocks South"

a sign posted at the corner of Maple & Main

I imagined how neatly their front sidewalk
would bifurcate possessions—
hers to one side, his to the other.
Instead, strewn across the lawn, they commingle,
one last time, plural on the way to single.
"Thank God there were no children"
someone who knows whispers.
But look at that orphaned steam iron,
the 4-slice toaster with frayed cord.
Seven frosted goblets suggest what?
The eighth dashed against a wall
in an argument, dropped
in the shock of surprise?
                              It's sad
how many early-birds quest heirlooms or antiques,
not nickel-and-dime bargains, and return to their cars
empty-handed. I feel compelled to buy,
to prove this spectacle to what-might've-been
still holds value. I reach past
a power drill, and from a chipped dish
pluck a tarnished spoon.
All this must be traumatic
for the woman taking my money.
                              Instead,
her posture, the toss of her head,
the eager way she makes change
says good riddance, says younger man—
clearer still, a new embraceable
independence. It's unexpected,

not anything I thought I'd glimpse
following a hand-lettered sign from the corner.
When I don't turn for my car,
she looks up from her cash box, inquiring.
So foolish in the face
of a longing I can't explain, all I manage,
holding up the spoon, is "Yours?"
"Was," she says, emphatic.

"Tidy"

after Rhina P. Espaillat

my friend's new lover says
of my house, my garden,
but meaning, I'm certain, me.
I might've endured "neat" or "orderly"
but "tidy" reeks of age, with desire
limned by duty and discretion,
is the roadblock to genius,
the cause behind disorder, syndrome, behind,
his look suggests, sexual repression.
Does a tidy person, he might as well ask,
ever get laid?

So, un-tidy-fy my life?
Unset the table, unmend the upholstery,
unplant the basil in its soldierly row
of pots on the sill? And if I were to toss
the sliced bread to the scavenging possums,
smash the clock's face, let trumpet vine
claim the porch, would someone—
he, for example—find me more appealing?

Tidily put, screw him.
I gladly live with the potential hazards
of stitched hems, matching socks,
of framed glossy photos, washed coffee cups,
the whir of wings against a snug screen.
I love to walk my discreet path
into the dark spruce of my hidden life
as clean sheets flap wetly on the line.

On Halloween

How innocent the seasonal question—
Who do you want to be?—
that once-a-year opportunity for re-invention.
How tempting to read too much
into my granddaughters' choices—
that Sarah, as bride, will marry early,
and Micaela, cheerleader, is doomed
to the sidelines. Let's hope
youngest Annie who demanded a "scary guy"
strikes out unafraid, ambitions ungendered.

Years from now, in some middle-age October
threatening to diminish the world leaf by leaf,
what tricks will they have they needed to master?
In some future autumn of life's afternoon,
might they lift from memory
their veil and pom-poms and mask
and ask, What other selves have my costumes hidden?

Oh may they then with exhilarated heart
recall how they quick-stepped into the dark,
their laughter shrill, on the edge, sweet-bags laden.
Let their imaginations leap from smolder to blaze
as they do this Hallow's Eve, seasons away
from sad arrangements, wrong turnings.
This night when anything seems possible,
when, frightened and giddy, little girls
of open minds and violable flesh,
venture forth in flimsy rayon and glitter.

"Slow Children"

Though none are in sight,
this yellow sign at the curb suggests
these are the streets
where the slow children play.
Where Larry at last moves
his desk to the front of the class
decades after we sat in second grade rows
the nuns ranked smart to dumb.
Here, no one runs
from Rudy with his flat, botched-chromosome face,
his lips loose, wild with spit.
Here, the cousins
who Cindy on her braces hobbled after
walk at a slower pace, don't zoom away
on their Schwinns.
The cheerful yellow sign opens its arms
to the narrows shoulders' slump, the moon face,
the useless, crooked legs.
In this neighborhood of bungalows,
of compact yards with swing sets, barbecues,
the sign says Welcome
to the brain's faulty linkage, to accidents
of chance, genetic predisposition.
Even the maples shade the sidewalks
in irregular patterns.

Forecast

"Morning fog will burn off by afternoon."
TV weather report

So thick, it seems unlikely,
this cottony vacancy I walk into, not one
visible boulder on the shoreline adding distinction.
Forget the bell buoy further out, the bridge
that tethers us to the mainland, or the other islands
similarly crowned with spruce.
This is a fog you can get lost in,
a fog that can swallow you whole, makes
the familiar unrecognizable—
it's easy to feel confused.
                                            Maybe
that's what my friend's father felt
in those days when memory first failed him,
when strangers began to inhabit
the bodies of his wife and daughter.
Something unbidden settled over him, heavier
than a scrim or sheet, deeper than sleep,
no matter how burning
his desire that it not be so.
                              What I know:
out there are boulders, bridge and island,
and back at my house, husband and dog,
connections that tie me to who I am.
They're gone now, but temporarily. Just listen
to how the waves keep on, their toss and flux,
as I pick my way in the tideline's wrack,
in what remains, is left behind.
                              My friend's father

still knows phrases in French,
his role in the War, the necessity
of utensils when eating mashed potatoes.
But she must introduce herself to him,
as if for the first time, again and again.

                         Imagine how,
at this moment, meteorologists bend over
their satellite maps and computer models,
the morning fog already receding
into memory, as they look to the future
and predict, with confidence, what comes next.

After Hearing about the Philosopher Who Moved Twenty-Eight Times in Seven Years

Imagine being that rootless, to move
each season, year after year, even from places

that had held such promise but soon lacked
the mountains he'd turned his back on

settling by the sea, or the quiet he'd refused
taking an address in the clamorous city.

He said he couldn't think—therefore did not exist –
without the proper landscape.

Such time it must've taken. Not the moving—
he owned so little—but the choosing.

And imagine the anxiety in continually believing
he'd picked poorly. No doubt

there was freedom, too, when impulse took over,
in escaping the snow or heat, a furious noise.

Would it sharpen wonder, the stimulus
of the always new, nothing ever too familiar—

no loaves set out to cool or fresh snow
shoveled from the bakery doorway,

no happy chatter of birds in the pines
or, beneath, a stream running clear,

or in the dark,
no feast-day fireworks over the seawall.

Perhaps it all winds up foreign,
wherever we reside. Strangers

in our final hours—not being where we are,
or where we are, not being.

III.

Dawn

The sun is suspended
in the spruce's lowest branches. No wind
has startled the oaks to rattle.
The only voices are the gulls', the warblers',
and nothing in their language
signifies to me expectation.

Oh, that I were capable
of such translation. To think
that because my eyes are now open,
I've put the whole thing into motion—
the oldsquaw's low tide probing,
the osprey's flight from its nest
of warp and sticks.
That because I throw back the covers,
step into my shoes, only now
will the road's curve beckon.

Like saying because the moon
has disappeared, she no longer exerts
her pull, and the sea needn't obey
its mistress. Like saying I bear no similarity
to flotsam, along for the ride.

Keys

All day I've made of our ordered house chaos.
My keys remain lost as though that's become
their business. A maddening mystery.
"Incomprehensible," I've shouted,
but that is stretching it. And in my angst,
so, too, the notion that these particular keys
represent the whole of my life's scatterings.
The dog, oblivious and shameless, tongues
his privates. A wren fidgets from branch to branch.
For them, what happens is what happens,
if that. For me, what will happen
does not exist yet. Meaning
my keys, as if by magic, might still show up,
or that I'll go to a certain pocket or shelf
as if divinely directed.
Meaning *lost* not *thrown away*
like certain opportunities. Meaning *lost* not *taken*
as stroke or cancer claim words or breasts.
Who would want the life of dog or wren,
days undifferentiated by yesterday or tomorrow?
No before-the-keys, no after-I-find-them.
Those places in between here and there,
between lost and gone.

The Body's Betrayals

Endless, the many ways the body betrays us:
a crippling stroke, a swift tumor,
a blighted lung or liver, the heart requiring a detour,

blood re-routed like traffic
through a congested intersection. The scene, perhaps,
of some prior accident, the wrecks

already towed to the side,
sirens bleating, those of us spared inching past,
our seat belts buckled, feet light on the gas,

but soon beyond,
our radios cranked full blast with all the noise
of the young who think themselves immortal.

Even in silence,
it's not possible to hear
patterns of cells re-arranging, the body

whispering its unmapped directions —
embolism, infarction, metastasis—
insistent as anesthetic,

while up ahead the road appears clear,
without hazard or fault in the surface,
no unexpected curve, no hidden exit.

Forget the Utopia

of childhood, gauze over lens, afternoons of cidery light,
the *thwack* of screen doors as dusk settles in.
I'll pause a moment though for the green
towering elms, all those domes
I rode my Schwinn beneath, pretending
myself a horse, my hair a mane, even if,
lank and thin, it was easily tamed
by a cheap barrette.

If I spare another moment, this one
for the pier at Cedar Lake,
let me only briefly mention
bronzed cousin Bonnie, slick as a seal,
or those summer afternoons of adolescence
when we began to think
we knew exactly who we are and little
can change it.

This, friends, is about the body my body
for years has wanted to become.
The one that doesn't refuse eyeglasses
or the fallen arches obedient to gravity.
So much for limbs trim as a colt's—
welcome upper arms and thighs
that say good-bye to tank tops and shorts.
Thin lips as easily as plumped
can form themselves around
whatever words they wish, or notes
not out of reach yet.

And here's to the still excitable eye,
to the territories of the mind, its wild imaginings,
and where I can so easily recall
how quickly dusk weighed in
as we wove our bicycles in and out
of lamp shine, and swallows winged home
to their hidden nests.
And those luscious pink tea roses
along our fence—for a few days, so near
their end, their blooms swelled
the size of clenched fists.

A Walk After Rain

In the puddles, on the sodden shoreline, my dog,
alive in complex networks of bone and sinew,
leaps, whirls, spins
a rambling sentence of paw prints,
odd scribbled letters easy to translate.
Like the three white horses at Edgewater salt farm,
heads lowered to the thick wet meadow.
Their faces and flanks in the after-storm shine,
say in such radiance,
in their refusal to come to the fence,
This is happiness.
                    If only
for the length of a morning walk,
I'd like to banish
my mind's nattering, its bruising knowledge,
the directives of an awakened conscience
to how I should've carried my silver pail,
collected berries for breakfast,
or how, if I was going to circle Dunham's Point,
I might've carried powdered doughnuts
to the island's newest widow.
I'd love to savor nothing more
than the swing of my arms, the ease
of my next breath and rhythmic steps, my heart
muscling my feet up the road.
                    But later,
when the sun is done purpling the Camden Hills,
and taped music replaces
all daylight falling over my face and ears,
how I would miss my brain's generous gifts,
the brilliance of my mind's supple choreography,

its intricate footwork to "Fascinating Rhythm,"
or the Olympian triple salchows I cut in the ice
to a Rachmaninoff concerto.
Supine on the couch, I don't have to lift a finger.
I don't even need to bow
to an audience wild with ovation.

Winter Kill

Some who saw swore
those dogs who chased a doe
onto the millpond's ice
were a bunch of rowdies, up to no good,
and who, once the doe was struggling and fell,
unable to rise, didn't finish
what they'd set out to do. I say
they answered dim ancestral calls
before heeding keener hungers
for bowl and hearth.
As for the eagle who the next morning
sank its head into the doe,
a carcass's fresh red slush,
no customary *noble* or *regal* applied.
Nor did the eagle oblige,
displaying moments akin to joy,
or of being sated and grateful for it.
Each day for a week the eagle returned,
indifferent to our cars slowing on the causeway,
ignorant of the conversation's main topic
beneath the Post Office's posted Ten Most Wanted,
as if a crime had been committed.
But we, too, are often urged forward.
We, too, can be brought to our knees. We feed.
And for all our words, we disappear
into unknowable silence
as surely as we flinch, attempt
to look away, inching across the causeway
or pulling into the millpond's turn-out,
and behind windshields, our breaths cloud glass,
each of us alone, separate.

Billions Populate the Earth

after Wisława Szymborska

And so few faces my life and its choices illumine.
Particularity, we're taught, matters. But truly,
how many features unique to a person
can I summon from Somalia or Rwanda?
Ditto the former Soviet Union, its republics
so unimaginatively and similarly suffixed,
their inhabitants rarely rendered
in pixels, through fiber-optics.
I've not mentioned the citizens
of China's far provinces, who, until this moment,
weren't so much as a blip on my mind's horizon.
You'd think I was blind
to the continent just south of us
or that it's necessary to go that far
to have imagination fail me.
When did I last consider our own country's
shifting boundaries between *enough* and *excess*,
indulge in just one of Appalachia's hungry children
or a dispossessed assembly liner in Detroit?
Sitting at my desk, not lifting a finger or turning a page,
it's as if I have minutes, hours starving
to be populous, but I tell you, no crowds
line up to clog my dreams.
Billions of people populate the earth
and I celebrate them, the faceless with their empty hands
and indescribable losses, who ask of me nothing,
who don't keep me from writing
the poem I've yet to finish, about how, you know,
in my kitchen this morning, and obviously no place else,

seen by no other eyes but mine,
there was a certain slant of light particulate with dust,
although now I'm trying to recall why
it seemed so urgent, why it matters.

So Many Depictions

of Madonna and the beatified saints,
but Vermeer sanctified light, the very light
that this morning enters my window,
lavishes with liquid gold my table,
its bowl of fruit, the fold of my sleeve,
and though I hold no pitcher of milk,
no balancing scales, and surely no Savior infant,
I feel blessed by this moment so ordinarily holy,

when time seems arrested
as in a master's landscape, when trees appear
to root beneath the oil paint, and clouds freeze
into singular shape. But no matter
how firmly I grip this table—
as if it were a canvas bolted into a frame—
light recedes, these plums
plums again, their souls mere stones.

The Season's First Apples

At the farmstand, among the crates
of late tomatoes and corn, the season's
first apples blush at their debut—

smooth, unmottled beauties too pretty to eat.
For days, the ones I choose
adorn my kitchen shelf, their stout stems

like perky caps, tams, perhaps,
the kind without protective earflaps.
At the open window, wind is disguised

in the stillness of trees, the luffing
sails in the harbor. Nowhere
in my radio's broadcast is there a forecast

of snow. I have no need
for socks or a sweater. But at the sound
of my first bite of the season's first apples,

boots crunch through icy layers.
Frozen tree limbs stutter
against the roof and gutters.

And the stove gapes open, ready
to make of another cord of wood
ash. How solitary

the flame of a single struck match
that on certain cold nights
seems like the only salvation.

Ice Cakes and Frost Heaves

At last, in today's brisk blast of onshore wind,
the cove, again, is wrinkling.
Tides stack ice cakes
once joined and thick enough to walk
to Crow Island, an illusion
of permanent connection, of no separation,
in the way, at times, our dogs
or even the deer nibbling windfall
do not seem entirely outside ourselves.
In the snow melt, landscape removes its bandages,
exposes new losses of winter-kill, blow-downs.
No dazzle or glint yet, all run-off and mud. Still,
Verne at the post office, Byron at the dump,
give evidence our blood, like sap,
has awakened, hums.
Temporary road signs—Heavy Loads Prohibited—
might as well exclaim
Welcome to the Season of In-Between, have faith
in what's-to-come, in the landscape behind this one –
hidden blooms, afternoons of insect monotones,
a welter of migrating birds, and here and there,
against an endless cloud-scribbled sky,
white tethered bed sheets that lift, rise,
looking, perhaps, to the believer's eyes,
like the wings of angels reluctant to leave.

Why Insist

In the maples, robins announce
their abrupt arrival—*Cheer up, cheerily*—
and in the spruce, arterial clots of cardinals –
Omit, omit. Oh, why insist
on vocalizing their music, the verbal
insinuation of human song?
Drink your tea, drink your tea –
odd admonishment
from a rufous-sided towhee.

It's all poor approximation anyhow.
Human language has its limitations.
Eskimo, for example, with its
twenty-six words for *snow*, not one
for *home*. No matter the number
of synonyms for *grief*,
which, if any, is ever adequate?

Who can say what the canary
in its ruffed throat is compelled
to sing about, sentenced
to a dark cavern far from familiar
branches cross-hatching blue?
Why translate its music
as anything other than struck match,
bituminous flame, or, for the miners,
a small, sweet consolation?

In this just-lit margin of morning,
its scattering shadows, birds raise
their virtuoso voices, chips of wild song,

and bring me the world—the saffron
smear of willow, early daffodils butter-yellow.
Even the common sparrow
whose whole body when it sings
trembles. How its reedy trills
seem to say in perfect syllables what I cannot.

Island Wave

after Wesley McNair

Two fingers raised from the steering wheel—
island greeting to friends, tourists,
neighbors passed every day, a gesture
that hasn't gone the way
of cod or herring seiners in the harbor.

And how I'd miss it, even though a wave
on the road can't tell me if Rich,
careening around the curve in his pick-up
just lost his job, or Margaret at her flagged mailbox
retrieves the news her tumor isn't benign.

Nor can it say if that kid on his bike
might be the next Andrew
who barefoot and wet in a thunderstorm,
sought shelter beneath a metal shed's overhang.
How fleeting those moments before

a hand raised in greeting becomes a good-bye,
the words implied—*See you soon, Call me*—
as Rich is lost to another curve, Margaret turns away,
envelopes clutched to her breasts, and that space
between us grows too vast

for words. Maybe too much is asked
of such a simple gesture.
Hello, good-bye, the connection we want to keep
at evening's end as good friends depart
beyond the porch light or as a sister boards a plane,

disappears into the ungirded sky.
Or yesterday afternoon, as a former neighbor and I
picnicked on the shoreline at Barred Harbor,
exchanged stories of kids and dogs and holidays
when our lives intersected on a shared country lane.

At our feet water lapped, the tide
insisting on its certainties,
its constant motion, constant change,
in every rise and fall
both approach and a going away.

How else, after that, to part,
conclude our afternoon, except with a wave,
its *Don't forget* the urgent request
of hands lifted against the moment
of our final taking leave.

In Crillon le Brave

after Charles Wright

Translucent dusk, and up here, above the cypress and cedar,
among the crenelated towers and red-tiled roofs,

swallows swoop toward our open windows,
then dart away with expert precision, as though stitching

limestone to sky, to backdrop of tilled hill and terraced vine,
needling, as clouds pass, day to night.

They're an irrefutable piece of this tapestried landscape,
but ignorant of it.

And of the invisible onlooker, too, who prowls
behind the constellations, threatens

to yank the cord on what-hasn't-happened-yet,
even on starless nights, the kind this waning light-wash

seems to be resisting. The way the natural world
seems to resist form—what had to be destroyed

to create this tidy village, its frescoes
and carved baptismal font?—but offers evidence

everywhere you turn of order.
How, abruptly as wind falls away, the swallows stop.

Heat retreats from August trees.
Another day wobbles on its trim green edge.

As night eases its way into my heart,
I can say the partial moon, tonight,

is half full. Knowing
the swallows will return at dawn,

I can say, believing it, nothing ends,
nothing is endless.

The Question

From an audible distance, the unseen owl inquires
Who are you? Who are you? Six syllables
mere lullaby, comfort, like the smell of balsam
through open windows, transformed, finally,
from question into suggestion—*Go to sleep. Go to sleep.*
You do not think about the question,
the way you do not think about a cloud
that no matter how splendid or vast
pushes past and never comes back, an immensity
removed yet tangible.

But wake at 3 a.m., gripped by something
you cannot name, all dreamscapes forgotten,
so many clouds passing in the dark unnoticed,
and *Who are you?* becomes
What have you done with your life?
Or say, the owl's syncopated intervals cease
into a particular, more frightening quiet, some mortal
extinction delivered by unerring wing.

At dawn, so weightless a thing as light
descends, and a warm wind from the Gulf
heaps nimbus on the horizon, stirs the birch leaves
so improbably counterclockwise.
With another morning of feeding the dog, opening the paper,
it's as if you've begun to answer.

Notes to Poems

"If a Single Word" is written after and derives its epigraph from "Home" by Eavan Boland.

"If Not Moonless" is written after Margaret Gibson's "Epistle to Gerard Manley Hopkins."

"Just One God" is written after and borrows its title from a line in Wesley McNair's "Losses."

"So Now I Have" is in response to "The Obligation to be Happy" by Linda Pastan.

"Meeting the Family" is written after Jan Bailey's "Rite of Passage."

"Tidy" is written after Rhina P. Espaillat's "For Evan, Who Thinks I'm Too Tidy."

"On Halloween" is for Carolyn, Hope, Micaela, Sarah and Annie.

"Forecast" is for Andrea Hollander Budy.

"Keys" is for Ted Kooser.

"Billions Populate the Earth" is in response to "A Large Number" by Wislawa Szymborska.

Line 4 in "Why Insist" derives from and "In Crillon le Brave" is written after Charles Wright's "Meditation on Song and Structure."

"Island Wave" is written after "Waving Good-Bye" by Wesley McNair.

Line 15 and an image in lines 8 and 9 of "The Question" are borrowed from "Waiting for Tu Fu" by Charles Wright.

Deborah Cummins is the author of a previous collection of poems, *Beyond the Reach* (BkMk Press). Her numerous recognitions include James A. Michener and Donald Barthelme fellowships, the Washington Prize in Fiction, the Headwaters Literary Prize, and multiple awards and fellowships from the Illinois Art Council. She has taught and led workshops at the University of Chicago, Northwestern University, Chicago Museum of Modern Art, Menil Collection in Houston, Texas, and Chicago's Terra Museum of American Art and Newberry Library. From 2001 to 2005, she was first Chair of the Board of the Poetry Foundation and currently serves on the board. She resides with her husband in Evanston, Illinois and Deer Isle, Maine.

Printed in the United States
78623LV00005B/439-465